A Funny Thing Happened After the Courthouse:
10 Things Learned About Divorce
Short & Simple Self-Realizations To Help Get Back on Track

Dr. T. D. Robinson

Copyright © 2015 Dr. T. D. Robinson

All rights reserved.

ISBN-10:0692575987
ISBN-13:978-0692575987

DEDICATION

This is dedicated to all those survivors of divorce. You made it!

CONTENTS

	Acknowledgments	iii
1	*Introduction*	5
2	*Self-Realization Number Ten:* Are you settling or did you settle?	8
3	*Self-Realization Number Nine:* Did you give up too much of yourself?	12
4	*Self-Realization Number Eight:* Independence isn't a bad thing	16
5	*Self-Realization Number Seven:* If you don't find Mr. Right, Mr. Right Now is okay	19
6	*Self-Realization Number Six:* His midlife crisis is not your fault	23
7	*Self-Realization Number Five:* God will always be there for you	27
8	*Self-Realization Number Four:* You will be okay	29
9	*Self-Realization Number Three:* Don't give up on finding happiness	31

10	***Self-Realization Number Two:***	34
	You find out who your true friends are	
11	***Self-Realization Number One:***	39
	There is life after Divorce	
12	***So What's Next?***	41

ACKNOWLEDGMENTS

I would like to first thank God from whom these words flowed. I would also like to express my deepest and sincerest appreciation to all the friends and family who supported me during what was a most difficult time in my life. I may have been smiling on the outside but you know the real me and was ever present even though I said I was 'okay'. Thank you, thank you, thank you! Last but not least to my husband, thank you for showing me that indeed there is life after divorce. You are the 'bestest'!

1
INTRODUCTION

The whole idea of marriage is perhaps one of every little girl's dreams that ranks right up there with being a princess. Whether you are the type enamored with everything from the wedding dress to the wedding cake or the type that likes simplicity when it comes to nuptials the entire wedding process can be a magical time. It can be an overwhelming experience that varies from one individual to the next. Nevertheless the one constant that remains is we all want the same thing: the happily ever after. The thought of divorce is nowhere in the picture perfect scenario.

Like many women living the fairy tale marital dream without warning I found myself divorced. Then again, could it be that like many women there were warning signs but I failed to see or did see but completely ignored the signs. Whatever the case experiencing a divorce when you thought that you were supposed to be living until 'death do you part' can be a devastating experience for many. You are left not only picking up the pieces of perhaps a life deferred but you may be left with so many questions. What am I going to do? Where am I going to go? What am I going to tell everyone because everyone thought we were the 'perfect couple'? Once you get over these and many more questions you will learn to focus on *you* and not the negativity that got you to this point. You may also learn a few other things along the way as well as perhaps come to some similar self-realizations that many women experience.

A funny thing happened after the courthouse. My eyes were opened to many things that I never realized had taken place when it came to marriage, life, and me. I decided to turn an uh oh moment into an aha moment. The following are some self-realizations that got me through what could have been a very difficult period in life. I hope these self-realizations will help and resonate with others experiencing this most difficult life event.

The overall realization for me was that for all of us unexpected life events such as divorce happens. When it does, we figure out how we got there, how to learn from it and move on, and work on ensuring that we don't end up in the same situation in the future. If we do find ourselves divorced again in the future, so what. Life happens!

2
SELF-REALIZATION NUMBER TEN: ARE YOU SETTLING OR DID YOU SETTLE?

As women many of us either dream of the day that someone says those four little words 'will you marry me?' or we avail ourselves to the fact that we may never hear those words. As such, often when we do hear those words no matter under which of the aforementioned circumstances we are so elated that we may overlook some very important factors. We are so caught up in the moment that we may ignore things that others may want to ask or that you should be asking yourself. Perhaps the one all-important question we should ask ourselves but fail to ask is 'Girlfriend, are you sure this is **THE** one?!'.

Often individuals get themselves into situations that over time they come to regret all because they may have settled or elected to let emotions take over rational thinking when it comes to relationships. That fantasy of the fabulous dress, cake, and wedding lead many to ignore the fact that the groom may not be fabulous. Something may be 'off' about your future husband but you minimize or ignore it because you are temporarily blinded by what I call the wedding glitter. Therefore, you may settle for the less than perfect groom because what becomes more important is that you get the perfect dress that accommodates your figure, the perfect venue to seat all those well-wishers who will come to see **YOU** and bring expensive gifts, or you become more concerned with it being **YOUR** day. Never do you question 'Am I settling?'.

The question of whether one settled for the person they married may come into play once all the glitz and glamour of the wedding has worn off and life begins to get real. This realization may really hit once you find yourself heading to divorce court. In the head-spinning aftermath of divorce that is one of the many questions I had to ask myself. Had I settled? Did I settle because this was the first person who proposed to me? Did I say 'yes' because I was afraid that no one else would ever propose to me again and I'm getting too old to be unmarried? Fortunately, I can say that I do not feel that I settled. That was the right person for me at that time and phase of my life's journey. Unfortunately, there are many who when asking themselves the question of whether they settled the answer will more than likely be 'yes'. Nevertheless, you know what, that's okay. Many commit to a marriage for a variety of reasons and settling may fall into one of those categories.

In our daily lives we all make mistakes or make decisions based on reasons that vary from those that are genuine to those that are superficial. Deciding whom to marry is no different. Some marry for love while some marry for riches. However, a large number marry because that is what's expected from family members or society. Marriage is viewed as that next step in one's life journey. As I often tell students, college isn't for everyone so seriously evaluate whether you are there because you want to be or because it is expected of you. I say the same thing about marriage. Marriage isn't for everyone.

Not everyone is wife or mom material. So seriously evaluate whether you are marrying because you want to be or because it is expected of you from one entity or another. One should come to this self-realization before committing to what could turn into a life unwanted. Then they would have settled on a mate and marriage because society or someone expected it of them. It may be a smarter decision to choose single over settling and save yourself a potential march down not only the church aisle but also the courtroom aisle.

3
SELF-REALIZATION NUMBER NINE: DID YOU GIVE UP TOO MUCH OF YOURSELF?

As the fog of the divorce proceedings begin to wear off the self-evaluation continues and may even start to go into overdrive. After coming to the realization of whether you indeed had settled or not settled you then may begin to get angry with yourself. You will no doubt go from being angry with your ex to being angry with yourself and will continue this ping-pong match until you become one with yourself and with your situation. That anger emanated from questions about where will you go and what will you do or come to be will practically haunt you.

One reason for this haunting may be because for so many years your identity was as wife and in some cases mother. The thought of whether you gave up so much to be that man's wife, that man's cheering section, mother to his children, and that man's everything will begin to take over your mind. It may be easier said than done but don't let it consume your every waking thoughts. Absolutely, it **WILL** consume you during the early phases but then you will eventually snap out of it. Know that you are not the only one who have or are experiencing such thoughts.

Often when we become man and wife we immediately and happily accept the traditional role of what a wife is supposed to be. We become the cook, the housekeeper, the caterer to his every whim, and eventually we become 'mommy' to him as well as literally becoming mommy. I don't know how we do it but we do so and very effectively I might add. With each additional label we take on we seem to get further and further from our own identity and needs. Everyone else's needs come before our own. This is especially true when it comes to putting our husband's needs before our own. This is done so often and for so long that what remains is a semblance of what we used to be prior to marriage.

Buried under these various identities is the former self that once existed. Don't get me wrong. These new identities one acquires are not necessarily a bad thing. All I'm saying is that we need to balance these new identities with our old identities.

There is nothing wrong with taking on additional titles in the relationship. Just remember when you go into a new relationship **NEVER** give up too much of yourself. Maintain your own identity. Not only will maintaining your own identity allow for you to be a better you but it will also make you a better person when you are dealing with all the other identities that you take on in the relationship. We have all heard the saying 'ain't nobody happy if momma's not happy'. If you give up so much of yourself that your life consists of only making everyone else happy, then you will eventually find yourself unhappy.

Another thing you might discover is you may perhaps find yourself unsatisfied because you are meeting everyone else's needs and not your own. This can be especially problematic if your needs are additionally not being met by your significant other. Who is going to take care of you if you don't take care of you? Other than perhaps your parents no one on this earth will ever love you as much as you love yourself. So love yourself and ensure that you continue to do things to maintain your happiness whether in or out of a relationship.

4
SELF-REALIZATION NUMBER EIGHT: INDEPENDENCE IS NOT A BAD THING

Once the divorce is done and you are metaphorically and literally divorced you will realize that being independent isn't such a bad thing. Sure it will be scary at first. The longer you were in a relationship the longer it might take you to adjust to your newfound independence. One reason for this may be that for so long you had to live as a couple and not as an individual and you behaved and were seen as a unit. Gone are the days where you couldn't make a purchase because you had to or felt the need to consult with your 'other half' prior to purchase. Nor could you just go hang out with the girls because you had to 'run it by' your spouse first. You are now an independent woman in control of your own thoughts, behavior, and actions.

Use this time to figure out what you want out of life, career, future relationships etc. Your newfound independence is a time to reconnect with ***the you*** that you used to know as well as explore new opportunities. Visit places that you've always wanted to visit, finish that novel you started writing eons ago, or start that business you've always wanted try your hand at. Heck, get wild and put the toilet paper roll on backwards the way you like it. The point is when it comes to you and your well-being you are the independent in charge of making decisions for you. All that I recommend is that you act responsibly. This isn't your time to get crazy and try to relive some wasted or forgotten youth. This is the time for you to reassess and take stock in what's important from here on out.

Use your newfound independence wisely. Your independence is not a time to sit around and sulk about what was, what is or what could have been. What's done is done, the check on that phase of your life has been cashed so move on. Use this time to reconnect with someone you may not have seen in quite some time: **YOU**! This might be the best and most trusted friend you may meet immediately following your divorce. This long lost friend will be very happy you decided to come around again.

Nurture this new friendship then reach out to other friends in your life that you may have put on the shelf while married. Be careful though! Only reclaim those friends who are and were true friends from beginning to end. Avoid those so-called fair weather friends and those who are negative. The last thing you need in your life at this point is negativity. As you are reading this you already have names of the negative know-it-all fair weather friends running through your head.

5
SELF-REALIZATION NUMBER SEVEN: IF YOU DON'T FIND MR. RIGHT, MR. RIGHT NOW IS OKAY

Ah, Mr. Right. That fictitious character we build in our mind and try to hold every man to such litmus testing. He has to look a certain way, he has to have certain material items, he must have certain qualities, and the list can go on for pages. Everyone is searching for that perfect specimen. Not saying that he is not out there but there may be a 99.9% chance that he doesn't exist. Not in any way discouraging you from searching for Mr. Right. Just warning to not end up settling for Mr. Wrong or overlook Mr. Right Now.

More than likely the existence of Mr. Right Now may be more probable. Once out that divorce hurricane often many quickly go on that search for Mr. Right because according to their diagnosis the ex turned out not to be Mr. Right. Therefore, you begin to go on that dating roller coaster in search of Mr.

Right only to find that he is Mr. Wrong or a Mr. Right Now. We don't need an explanation as to what is wrong with Mr. Wrong……but what is wrong with Mr. Right Now? Doesn't Mr. Right Now deserve a chance?

In the quest for Mr. Right we may toss away a potential Mr. Right Now because he isn't Mr. Right. Be cautious in doing so because there is nothing wrong with Mr. Right Now. How do you know that he isn't going to develop into a Mr. Right? In other words, don't simply discount someone because they don't fit every criteria that is on that dream man list you comprised. **NO ONE IS PERFECT NOT EVEN YOU!** So stop expecting everyone else to be perfect. You didn't expect perfection with the mate you divorced so why are you expecting it so highly from future mates?

The search for perfection appears to be a pattern that many follow when a relationship ends. For example, because the prior relationship didn't work you may say it didn't work 'because he wasn't Mr. Right'. Therefore, you declare that you are going to make sure that the same calamities don't happen again. To ensure such doesn't happen, you comprise a list of characteristics your new mate must possess. You also swear to all that you are going to stick to that list no matter what. Isn't it funny how we develop standards after our failed relationships? Where were these standards prior to entering a relationship or a marriage? Perhaps these desired characteristics in a mate are suppressed by the idea of 'I'm no longer single, I got a man!', the engagement ring, an impending marriage and the wedding glitter.

Give Mr. Right Now a chance. It's okay because there is simply nothing wrong with taking it slow and exploring Mr. Right Now because you never know he could turn out to be your Mr. Right. If he turns out to not elevate to Mr. Right status it's still okay because again, no one is perfect so compromise and adjust your list. If you decided that you do not wish to remain single you are going to have to adjust your list. A decision needs to be made as to what are the things you can live with as well as those things that you simply cannot. However, do not downgrade your Mr. Right list to the point that you are settling just to avoid being single. Remember: choosing single over settling may save you future heartache.

6
SELF-REALIZATION NUMBER SIX: HIS MIDLIFE CRISIS IS NOT YOUR FAULT

Often after a lengthy marriage that ends in divorce one of many reasons a woman may find herself in divorce court is because her beloved hits that dreaded thing called a midlife crisis. Denial may be the immediate response by many and the denial may continue as he's standing there looking at you a 40 something year old dressed in trendy hip hop clothing that a 20 something year old would wear.

Others may come out and admit they are going through some type of crisis where they feel that they need to start a new life and that can only be done without you in the picture. While yet some others may exhibit the stereotypical behavior we have all come to know as signs of a midlife crisis. You know those types that go out and get the flashy car and the new girlfriend that looks young enough to be his daughter. However, keep in mind not all midlife crisis involve the stereotypical scenario of the husband leaving the devoted older model for a younger model.

Be prepared to hear what I term miscellaneous 'cop outs'. For example, statements such as 'there has to be more to life than going to work and paying bills' or 'I wanna go see what's out there' may be common phrases you might hear. Nevertheless, whatever reason that is given, you know that there is a midlife crisis going on because you see it even if he fails to see it. One thing you must realize is that his midlife crisis is not your fault.

Certainly you may know about the signs and probably have been seeing them for quite some time but ignored or justified them away. Is it your fault? Should you have addressed the subtle changes that were occurring? Should you have been doing something to prevent ending up in your current situation? The answer is emphatically NO!

As women in relationships, we often see things that are not working out as being our fault. We shoulder the burden of why things don't go right when it comes to others. This is something we need to stop doing but we can't help it because we naturally are nurturers and have a tendency to want to fix things. When it comes to a midlife crisis, you cannot change, control, or eliminate the crisis. You also need to accept that perhaps part of the reason you can't do anything about the crisis is because underlying issues may exist and it may not be about you.

Undoubtedly, you may be told that the reason for wanting an out is because of you (something you're doing or not doing) but trust that there may be more going on beneath the surface. More than likely you will never truly learn what that is because it's easier to place blame on someone else rather than soul search or admit fault with one's self.

What you need to keep reiterating to yourself is that you cannot control another individual's behavior. Sure we love to think that we can control others but we only control as much as they let us control. Keeping that thought in mind, whatever midlife crisis he may be going through know that this is simply something out of your control. This is his to sort through on his own with or without your assistance. He will have to eventually deal with his issues.

If that happens either you come to some sort of happy medium and work things out or you make the decision to amicably, hopefully, part ways. If you are reading this book, the parting of ways has more than likely occurred. Don't fret! His midlife crisis may have gotten you to this point in your life but his midlife crisis is not your fault…..no matter what he says.

7
SELF-REALIZATION NUMBER FIVE: GOD WILL ALWAYS BE THERE FOR YOU

Isn't it funny how it seems that whether religious or not when we feel that we have nowhere else to go and no one else to turn to we always call on God. Now I say God because that is the higher power I look to for spiritual guidance. Whomever you depend on to water your spiritual garden, know that your spirituality will be there for you always.

Even when we fall by the wayside as they say when things get tough we always seem to find our way back to our spiritual base. If you don't have a strong faith base perhaps now is the time to reintroduce yourself to Him. If you currently have a strong faith base, continue with that strength and rely on others who share that same spirituality to get you through this difficult time.

God is love and God loves you even when you don't love yourself at the moment or think that no one else loves you. Perhaps this individual was not whom God meant for you to continue your life's journey. Perhaps as stated earlier this was the person that God placed in your life for this particular season in your life. You may not see it at the time because you are emotionally broken but trust that everything happens for a reason.

We do not know God's plan or design for our life. Be still and listen to Him and let Him guide you to your next journey. Not only in relationships but in every aspect of your life. I am a firm believer in the old adage that God doesn't give us more than we can handle.

8
SELF-REALIZATION NUMBER FOUR: YOU WILL BE OKAY

What am I going to do? How am I going to survive? Will I make it? Am I going to be okay? These are only a few of the many questions you are going to ask yourself as you go through your recovery period. You are not the first and definitely won't be the last to go through such an emotional event in life. In fact, once you get through this you will realize that this wasn't the great tragedy in life that you thought it was at the time.

Sure it was emotionally devastating, some financially devastating, and we don't need to say that it was also heartbreaking. Nonetheless, we all get through it and once we get back on our feet we realize it was not the 'go play in traffic' moment that we gave so much of our time and energy to at the time.

Hearts mend, emotions eventually are reeled in, and finances soon become a non-factor. We recover and we often come out tremendously wiser and more in control of our lives. We begin to see things for ourselves that we couldn't see before because we were totally giving our all to one individual and not taking care of ourselves. Remember a few pages back I talked about giving up too much of yourself in the relationship?

You will be okay in this life event similar to any other event in your life. Remember that job you lost and fretted about what were you going to do, where were you going to go, or how were you going to pay your bills? You found another job, right? Perhaps even a better paying and more rewarding job than the one you just lost. The same will happen to you with regard to a relationship. You may just get lucky and find a better and improved relationship. Again, everything happens for a reason. Believe and live that mantra!

9
SELF-REALIZATION NUMBER THREE: DON'T GIVE UP ON FINDING HAPPINESS

"That's it!!!!! I'm done with men!!!!". Isn't that what we all say when a relationship sours? You may really mean it at the time and perhaps even need a break. That's fine and definitely recommended so that you can find the **YOU** again that I spoke of earlier. It's also fine because you need to clear your head and focus on getting yourself together and preparing for the journey ahead. Use as much time as possible or as you need to re-gain your identity, reintroduce yourself to **YOU**, and simply **BREATHE**.

You can't make anyone else happy or share happiness if you're not happy. Find happiness in yourself before you go out to find happiness. Don't let your happiness be defined by who you are with, by things, or by the things whomever you are with may possess or gift to you. So many fall victim to finding happiness in others or things and not finding happiness within themselves. Happiness begins with you and **ALWAYS** look for that happiness within yourself. Don't let anyone define your happiness. Also, don't let them determine what will make you happy. Are they sharing your brain and that qualifies them to tell you what will make you happy?

You will have many armchair relationship experts in your ear telling you they have been through a similar situation. These armchair therapists or as I call them armpit therapists may even go as far as to suggest what they did to get through the situation and suggest you do exactly as they did. However, just because that worked for them will not necessarily work for you because individuals and situations are different. Although on the surface the situations may appear similar but once you peel back the layers you discover they may be quite different. You know how you and your best friend both wear size 8 shoes but they fit each of you differently for whatever reason? Or you wear a size 10 jeans by one designer but a size 10 jeans by another designer fits you like a size 6. The same can be said about situations, especially relationships.

Therefore, when that girlfriend says 'Girlllllllllllllllllllllll I have been there and here's what I did and this is what you should do!' just smile. Kindly listen to her advice because you may in fact be able to utilize some of her advice if you think it's applicable. However, I reiterate that you should remember that what worked for your friend may not necessarily work for you. You are two entirely different persons, personalities, and your situations if explored deeper contain different variables. Don't give up on happiness within yourself or happiness with another mate because everyone deserves to be happy. You will find that happiness in a relationship again. So don't give up because your other half or soul mate as some like to call it is out there waiting for you.

10
SELF-REALIZATION NUMBER TWO: YOU FIND OUT WHO YOUR TRUE FRIENDS ARE

If you really want to shorten your friends list and can't quite seem to decide on who to delete, just go through a life event such as a divorce or needing financial help. You will find out real fast who your true friends are. Even more eye opening is that you find out that those who you thought were your friends were actually the ones behind the destruction of your relationship. Just like everything is clear once you are out of the center of all the madness so will the issue of who is or isn't a friend will become very apparent.

When I was going through my divorce, I had a small core group of friends who I believed all were there for me. All but one turned out to be genuine friends. This truly was a shock to me because that individual was closer to me than perhaps all the other friends. Well, while I was going through my situation and sharing all of my plans with regard to the divorce proceedings she and her husband were reporting everything to my soon to be ex-husband. Which when I found out totally surprised me because she was my friend and only knew my husband because of me. Had I not always been one step ahead when I went to court the entire proceedings could have turned out disastrous for me.

Of all the friends this was the only 'friend' that started to pull away and rather than support me became distant. This was someone who purported to be a Christian. She stopped inviting me to her house (I later found out she and her husband were inviting my soon to be ex over for dinner....primarily to feed him information she'd gotten from me.) and stopped accepting invites to my events. I just assumed it's like some married friends get when a friend becomes single. One of those situations where they don't want their single friend around because they fear the friend might try to take their man. I was baffled because she knew that I didn't want her man for a long laundry lists of reasons. Heck, she shouldn't even want her man. I could write a book or two on that relationship.

Long story short, she was painting me as this evil entity to my soon to be ex-husband and encouraging him to divorce. She even convinced him that all of our other friends were also the devil. Years later my ex and I discussed this and I asked him how he could listen to that pair. Primarily because they are the most dysfunctional toxic married folks we know and she should have left her husband eons ago because of the way he treats her.

All of our friends have witnessed the maltreatment of this individual who we called 'friend'. Maybe she secretly was envious of my relationship and that's why she inserted herself into my relationship with the sole purpose of creating havoc and destruction once she saw a potential fracture. Who knows for sure. However, one thing I know for sure is that everyone that you think are your friends may actually be your frenemies.

Once out of the divorce and all the drama and emotions subsided my ex-husband realized that he should not have listened to the frenemies. He continued by saying that he even planned to call the entire divorce off until he got a phone call from the two of them talking about me to the wee hours of the morning. Funny, I told him he knew me for 14 years and this dysfunctional toxic pair for less than 4 years and he believed them? I guess some folks are very convincing and others easily convinced.

After the divorce was over, about a year later, this 'friend' started coming back around acting like nothing even happened and trying to be close like we were the best of friends again. To this day, she does not know that I know every single detail of what she did. I keep her at a distance and I know it kills her that I share no important details with her about my life. Even acquaintances know more about what's going on with me than she does. Through acquaintances is often how she finds out anything about me. What is it that they say you should do with friends and enemies? Well, if she reads this I guess she will now know that I have always known what she has done. All I can say is look out for karma.

Oh yeah, true friends. I can now call seven individuals (you know who you are) from my married days unequivocally my true friends. I can count on these true friends to be fair and balanced. These friends didn't take sides in the divorce and even tried to support my soon to be ex-husband but he shunned them because of that so-called friend and her husband.

These true friends I know are my ride or die friends that I can count on whenever the going gets rough. These will be the seven friends that if I won lotto tomorrow I wouldn't hesitate to share some of the winnings. Even my ex-husband and I remain good friends because he is truly a good person. Genuine friends are hard to come by so if you find them treasure them and guard them like the precious jewels they happen to be.

11
SELF-REALIZATION NUMBER ONE: THERE IS LIFE AFTER DIVORCE

Good true friends and family are vital in your life before, during, and after your divorce. If you have those, you are well on your way to 'recovery'. I didn't include family on my list of ten things because that's a given. You don't need a self-realization about family because family will always be there for you. No matter how dysfunctional or crazy they may be they will always be there for you when things go wrong whether you need them or not.

Whether we seek their input or not family will always be there for you. Just as a good religious or spiritual foundation is necessary to get out of your emotional turmoil having a strong family base is vital even if you only seek support from one or two family members.

There is life after divorce. Simple as that. The type of life you have depends solely on you and what you want to achieve and the direction in which you desire to go. The world is yours and you are capable of taking it by storm should you choose to do so. Nothing can stop you. If you have made it through this scary thing called divorce you can take on any of life's other big challenges. This is your life. This is your season.

Get out and experience new and exciting things. Look forward not back. Don't be unable to see your future because you still have the cataracts of the past. Again, don't let the divorce or any stigmas of being a divorcee define who you are and what you want to be in life. So go live the best you and get the best life possible for yourself. **Shine! Soar! Go get more!**

12
So What's Next?

I will tell you what's next. You are going to go out there and live life to its fullest and be absolutely fabulous while doing it! Many people sit around and mourn a divorce as if it is a death. Sure it's the death of a relationship but it is not the death of you! Get back out there and live! Don't let one situation or one person taint your belief in the idea of that happily ever after.

Moreover, don't let finding that person whom God has earmarked for you as your perfect fit be tossed aside due to your failed past relationships. Furthermore, for goodness sake when you find that new relationship please **DON'T** commit any of the following most common behaviors (this by no means is an exhaustive list):

1) Bring divorce 'baggage' to a new relationship
2) Compare this new person to your ex

3) Assume this person will do the same as your ex
4) Constantly bring up old issues from the past or talk about your ex
5) Depend on this new person for your happiness
6) Completely give up all of yourself to this new person
7) Expect the new person to be perfect
8) Have the 'I'm going to hurt him before he hurts me.' attitude
9) Have trust issues
10) Expect the new person to live up to unrealistic expectations

This is your new beginning for the next phase of your life. This is your new season. Leave all the hate, anger, and any other negative emotions related to your divorce behind and see life's bigger picture. Leave all the negative individuals behind as well. Remove anything and anyone that's negative from your vocabulary and from your life in order to maintain positive clarity. You need that clarity in order to see what God has in store for you. You can't see it if those once clear and sparkling wedding glittered eyes are now experiencing divorce cataracts. Remember, when it comes to life: **Shine! Soar! Go get more!**

ABOUT THE AUTHOR

Dr. T. D. Robinson is a professor in higher education who resides in the southern U. S. with her husband and toddler children. Dr. Robinson writes on a wide variety of topics that range from professional and academic books and papers to more personal literature such as life experiences and children's literature.

www.ingramcontent.com/pod-product-compliance
Lightning Source LLC
LaVergne TN
LVHW051205080426
835508LV00021B/2818